A Reddish Sky

A Reddish Sky

David Heathcote

Copyright © 2020 David Heathcote

The moral right of the author has been asserted.

Apart from any fair dealing for the purposes of research or private study, or criticism or review, as permitted under the Copyright, Designs and Patents Act 1988, this publication may only be reproduced, stored or transmitted, in any form or by any means, with the prior permission in writing of the publishers, or in the case of reprographic reproduction in accordance with the terms of licences issued by the Copyright Licensing Agency. Enquiries concerning reproduction outside those terms should be sent to the publishers.

Matador
9 Priory Business Park,
Wistow Road, Kibworth Beauchamp,
Leicestershire. LE8 0RX
Tel: 0116 279 2299
Email: books@troubador.co.uk
Web: www.troubador.co.uk/matador
Twitter: @matadorbooks

ISBN 978 1838595 456

British Library Cataloguing in Publication Data.
A catalogue record for this book is available from the British Library.

Printed and bound in Great Britain by 4edge Limited
Typeset in 10pt Sabon by Troubador Publishing Ltd, Leicester, UK

Matador is an imprint of Troubador Publishing Ltd

Foreword

A Reddish Sky is a reflection of love lost, unrequited and fulfilled, with historical example, plus the reminisce to those who we have found and loved, lost or left. Distant friends and some who seem to sometimes, still appear daily.

Earth and its uniqueness also features as our ancient home with a few examples, of her priceless diversity, conceived of in another era of park sunsets in Reddish, Stockport.

But, in the words of a German Proverb, "Am morgen geht die sonne auf, und am abend geht sie unter." ("In the morning the sun rises and in the evening it sets")…It Changes! It always changes.

Come the day, perhaps, when after knowing and experiencing these simple yet complex milestones of people and discovery we are reminded and see them from the perspective of the journey to a reddish sky.

David Heathcote

Contents

1 – Beforetime	1
2 – A Reddish Sky	2
3 – Another's Tale (The Waterless Road)	3
4 – Anna Of Waters Edge	4
5 – Premier Amour	6
6 – Remember	7
7 – Spaceship	8
8 – Eden's Smile	9
9 – The White Willow	10
10 – Terra Incognita	11
11 – Lady Helen	12
12 – Araby	13
13 – Star Differs	14
14 – Mary R	15
15	16
16	18
17 – Fotheringhay	19
18 – Bharatavasha	20
19 – Gypsy	21
20	22
21 – The Five	23
22 – The Farewell	24
23 – Kanata	26
24 – Needless To Say	27
25 – Writing On The Wall	28
26 – Velvet	29
27 – All That Ventures	30
28 – Quiet Eilidh	31
29 – Scent of a Bottle	32
30 – To Find In The Ashes	33
31 – Secret Heart	34
32 – Wedding Day (The Crossing)	35
33 – Voyage (Who Will Mourn)	36

1 – Beforetime

Once the dappled tigers reign
Solitary, Lord of Indian night
Stripes of hunter, pads of plunder
Pounced of black before you came
Once reigned chaos, hard, commanded
Thumbs down by Roman Populaire
Arena led, to lions fed
Or Spartan training, pagan rule
Before this first hand, war obtained
Bodies to The Valley of Hinnom thrown
There, battles of an Empire fought
But in pain of crowds you saw, you took
In rendezvous are tyrants slain
And the glory of Emperors pale to dusk
In a song of songs, this Solomon's
And the time to slay the all beforetime
Is our time, arrival, in this moment now.

2 – A Reddish Sky

The Elms and Poplars, late November
That dressed in byegones sentries tell
Call and churn despaired December
For swings and roundabouts dispel
And watching these we walk and sigh
Our pilgrims trek to the Reddish sky

Once to our port, their starboard turned
'Though leagues from countries violent shores
Let more these souls, their faces burn
And sail to our memories haunt, the more
Let Pierrots tears splash ruins high
And reminiscence Reddish sky.

And who could reach for all our days
When wisdom, shouts from roofs aloud
This hall of mirrors, raptures gaze
The thousand, watching, listening crowd
Try we must – away and fly
To castle towers Reddish sky.

Must they who search for pearls not sleep?
Or travelling merchants sing of joy
In hearts own Counsel, waters deep
Let these discerning power employ
Let precious Kingdoms, none deny
Superlative, this Reddish sky

The playgrounds soak to winters truth
Where spun the endless shouts of May.
Against the collar turning proof
Of elemental forces way
But in this House of Days we lie
With ships that pass to a Reddish sky.

3 – Another's Tale
(The Waterless Road)

Too high, too far, never held, or to be
For mendicants low of desperate street
A nowhere road, empire of air
Gaze forlornly at hand in hand
Who forged beyond their destitute
Of powers, expressions of courage said
In eulogies, goddesses, gods who
Came and placed with angels, and over
Mere and love struck child of grief
Who wakens to burden of their day
Who stare to the vista, the never to be
Their cynosures, the never to see
With hunger that gnaws under howling of night
Their vision in falsest wrecking lamps
So crushed are terms of desert heart, lost
Thus stories of lustre, poppies shed
Keep walking this faith of petals to end
For a fairy tale told, but another ones tale.

4 – Anna Of Waters Edge

Moons ago once awaited spring
Touched over the heath of longings tide
Well nigh sunrise peered to smile.
To spatter eloquent waterside
And here moons ago each day was she
Who left by age of twenty three

A silken band, a delicate tinge
Sprung into Vervain copse
The break of light, Anna to waters edge cast.
Deigned to tarry for a family name
And village all but given to yield
The daughter tripping joyously unto silver fields

There the sunlight above, a sun below
A hart, then features invaded by dark
And wonderful tresses, under black branches
Over morning mirror, under sycamores lark
Off into the forest world, the gossip of the jay
Bereaving fear the hart and hares and Anna once gave play.

Such company to left, the solitary to right
Because through dancing revelry, emptiness's sound
The birds, the pawing beasts, those angels swift of day alone
For where one continues paradise is all but found
See a rippled shimmer, see the painted cheeks upon
See clearness under overhang, in burn the spectral one.

Still the Vervain copse, still treetop realm above
Banish of the Ice Queen, all awake to earths new touch
Again, a mirrored sky and branches yet
No tresses under sycamore, no waters edge, beloved touch
Alone the creatures kind, the jay, the hares, the prancing roe
At twenty three, to a heart anew was Anna moons ago.

5 – Premier Amour

Unto visions vainly tried.
The something of despair inclined
In moving hills, departs at the last
To premier strangeness, this so new
Do dreams return to they once passed
Or dreamers never know the true.

Words of virtue grow in stain
Wished no hurt, too high to be
And from all, never to see
Nor discern the pride, the fear.
Like Persian Laws our hope flees hard
Thin line reasons, still of the blind
Did once seem and not discard
The Reach, first and desperate kind
Answers answerless and there
To smile again unbowed to feel
From visionaries once are left nowhere
Amok times past amour unreal
As players leave their scenes until
Despaired December trees are still

6 – Remember

The ghosts who walked with us have met
In hold, in reach, to resurrect
Shrines of days and mortal woe
Fondest angels bright halo
This mirrored palace, here then gone
For we are the Legion, printed on
In prison binding, called afar
With love that stays its hand in ours
And make these loves that never doubt
As knowledge of high places shout.
Unnatural are the tragic hearts
Decrepitude's slow thief imparts.
A thief is king until he's caught
"And there's no god" the fool reports
So their always countenance.
The spectres floating provenance
From shuttered to unlocked and called
Their myriad of Autumns fall

7 – Spaceship

Through arid, through teeming celestial night
Who robed as a Queen is in time lost renown?
This speediest arrow, Spaceship flight
Superior diamond, never lost crown
Who but earth, bathed solar of fire again
Turns face to a morning of loving unfold
She crashes and smashes, her finishing when?
Cascades and her hauntings of night are not told
Great Trades for the treasure, spices of pleasure
Delta and tundra, palace of the range
Great trains ply the ways for ancients of days
Degrees, twenty three and half for the change
In shaded and danger, in tropical wind
Clear crystalline speaks to the ferny and wet
Bands of the desert are the gold of her rings
In slender life cloak, earth could we forget?

Every misted and sacred needle to shine
And words of a brave Suqamish outpour
Whatever befalls this world, in kind
Her sons, her daughters will there too befall.
Who reins in moving ships, sailors of a sealess
Shore of no tide, where lands of no one
Could last Arabian caravans, windsong more
And last rays low stoop to their time dressed son?
Be racing to frigid Australis's, dance
To no more its Southern performance of love?
An Orient and Occidents kiss would enhance
From worlds upon a world to Polar above
And below, the ice-kings despots' behest.
Continents forested, house millions yet
She in uniqueness, gifted, troubled one lest –
Spaceship of billions, we could forget.

8 – Eden's Smile

To a garden of stars, we reverie found
To stand at twilight and whisper awhile
We echoed earths past amid rapturous sounds
And the daybreak arose, the light of your smile.

For a pearl of great value a merchant once sold
His all acquisition for this to obtain
Like wondrous discoveries, riches untold
In a second you were this desirable gain.

Hard days you have gone are mere fountains of words
That elusively spring to poor artisans style
These thousands you are, the golden day heard
Could words ever match such skylighting smile.

Yes lyrics, verse, prose you are, a locked for many pages
Eternal pipers tune in Spring, this siege to all despair
A warmth that all invading, breeze of sighs pervading
The riot through a rain of storms transfixes every care

So to a Promised Land ahead we trod
And moon fall infinite, you were the piquant ray of youth
More worthy than the diamond eye upon a foreign god
Oh bonny lark, was more beauty ever found in truth.

So in the fire of raiment night is more elation found?
All vaunted wealth of Orient, persons simply would revile
And who would not forsake the golden crown
For you the prized, for Eden's touched these moments in your smile.

9 – The White Willow

Peer to the growths of the regal willow white
Harken to the eloquent, calling night
Hear the flagrant recollections, echo of the truth
The tumult, their rising in spring of heady youth

A twinkling dance of Kinderszenen, heyday there of joys
Years of the hillsides, here was the boy
In characters child, the girl elation wild
From flights of the immortal ones, childhood beguiled

White Willow arises of black skyline
Sorrowless and fords ascending time
Their voices played, when days were long
Below deep populations song

Hearts too fly and daystars see
The colours of night, let the white willow be
The solitary one, when he and country girl
To wonderful roads of the painted worlds.

In the memories of the evening's backcloth, stately, deep hung blue
There lives the comely willow, sits there the rise into
His openings, bathing faithful, fading, living past across
Clover, ling of generations, redolence of loss

The carpet brownness that lays siege to this, the autumn willow
Liberated hosts to scatter emptiness's pillow
Brother – Sister born of freedoms arms, in sacred home
Where the phantoms tarry, a White Willow mourns alone.

10 – Terra Incognita

Australis Incognita, Titan dressed of pearls
Anointed spirit in rock and in air
And ages, worships Dream
A heartbeat Nullarbor beneath
Sweet Nothing beats above there
Bestirring killing lands lifeforce
Bites, and stings – she crushes, crawls
To kill over waves of heartland heat
Ulluru's denizens flee or feed
At midday bake, Disappointment lake
The Queens own lush, the Arnhem bush
In Adelaide, sips Utopian wine
And breathing Pacific necklace, east
This unique coral country in reef
Superlative house for a family marine
A pageant beneath, black menace on high
Once locked there to Captains cabin and drawer
Were orders in shadows, precious of search.
So reach ahead terra enigma and known
O great southern sought, discovery at last.

11 – Lady Helen

Gently descending
Those locks and bow sending
This soul to a skyline
So perfect, unbending.

Endearment are you
When the foreseen is true
When all has forsaken
Fail not to race through.

Hither and tranquil
With soothe the cup fill
Lady Helen of secrets
To transport-and will.

In portraits to find
In an instance of sign
We travelling through outlands
With ancients of time.

To be worth all endeavour
To years and forever
To the paradise seas
Desert, we can never.

12 – Araby

The spoken deeds of heroes left
Waves of enigma, dunes bereft
Romance the idylls, steel clash
Those of the faith are the raindrops splash
The true believers, like stars in the cool
Where Arabian night and whims of rule
And Sultans stealthy, silhouettes came
The time-lined Lords of camel trains.

On the wind-coaxed crest, a Prince he stands
Whose burning slits descry the sand
Side to enduring beast alone
In breath of the zephyrs lonely roam
There the Chosen of the light and blessed
Princely charm, the hero zest
Who sped their cloud into the still
A trail and tale of the furrowed hills
Rare jewels, so ostentatiously
The visions of a shifting sea.

13 – Star Differs

When light has bled
When home is bed
When glories behind, above and ahead
That shimmer of years
To freely appear
And spangle eternity, night endear

And backcloth hue
A sombred blue
Contrast, the mercurials speed through
So vast from home
Their journeying lone
Their mystic barely touched or known

A dwarf pales white
Long aeons year light
Red and colossi in power incite
We peer to their past
Are human amassed
People of night blink bonny, so fast

Star differs from star
So stellar we are
In loneliest vigils night without par
So here all the more we
To chaos or glory
Sojourn to our order, the consummate story.

14 – Mary R

"O Northern Main by seaboard grey
My fated company, ye ken
Wi' breeze and heed the gulls cry not
Ye call for our lassie, beloved moorhen
For faiths sake Lord, stay sails on line
For surging my kin's hearts, aw' skip n' dance
Forever the heather and doon the deep glen
And souls to thee, Our Lady frae' France".

And pipes wail wide, 'cross moor and tide
Scepter and cord are gone.
Yield the night will, in surrender
Sigheth, when dawn breathes quietly on.

All days that patiently arrive
When hearts fall shadowed, who can tell?
Wherein there, tenderly resides
To kneel with quietly, one who fell
But amid their desperate warring bands
Will the warm winds that embrace thy heart
So surely pale to the crescent moon
Or turn, to the gale of adversities start.
"Then Adieu, Henry, my Lord, My own
When youth's eyes spoke so soon to fail
You were all and now by hands to rest
The overcast altar, once-again veil
How past still grows, the river aflow!
To stir and how your suffering, mine.
But scorn untoward my destiny shared
I curse and mourn men's vile design.

15

Upon thy moist cheeks, sanguine then
Ill-mask to their sword of ambition, prey.
Where Highland skies shall shift and pour
So truly love must whisper away
"My tears are wrung to stain thee delight
Evoke again so oft'
Didst I espouse, rekindle the years
Of twittering court or widows cloth
But vain spring fair Caledonian winds
A desolate promise of nought. allied
To the fortunes and hearts of fools so art
Thee thrice lost – yea familiar goodbye.
My plaintive cries who heard, this lake
Across where nights, the longest ones
I lay awake where company makes
A needle fly through whispered tones".

For whom lies barren, whose comfort gaunt?
Whose fruit may sweetly to the seasons blow?
When ripe and fine art plucked and
Cast – then hither crushed to the southward go.
With burn, their dire complicity
With thirst, oh thy revenge in full
Does refuge beckon to these shores
England 'cross the waters dull?
Or realm of inscription close to thee lies
'Though broad the theatre beyond will stay
The great hand now, for Queen of eyes
That haunt , beguile this land in gaze.
In conduct holy may you endear
Or endure while a rule shall long away bide
In years of wane, tomorrows love
Will faraway touch the distant tide.
" My Duke and the last, I pray lest
Are windward scattered dreams in sand
I take this diamond, hold thy words.
And just as surely take thy hand.
Remember our promised, conceived to the dust
'Though late may men sojourn – but I
As thee our eventide discern
Erstwhile was faith, mine now supply."

16

When virtues of the adverse ring
And echoed gates on foreign walls
Where a longed for Son and King
Once, triumphs recollection calls
But now the Puritan face a-stare
And prisons of accusing land
Insuperable who bring to bear
A Prophets malediction hand.

See flames are a-dance, listen, the hearth
Of a hall, or a stage, look so many frowns
And low now, eyes of silence behold
For whom thee concerns the mission of a crown
For cam' ye Lass 'till a scarlet rose
Lies torn and still in the blooded snow
Of a grey Februaries beginning with end
And the dearest sacrifice of Winter, below
The battlements sighs of morning where Mary
The stormy harvest reaps, for love of god today,
Thy peace Mary, at last, there in
The hall of Fotheringhay.

And pipes wail wide, 'cross moor and tide
Sceptre and cord have gone.
Yield the night will in surrender
Sigheth – when dawn breathes quietly on.

17 – Fotheringhay

This velvet night
That calls in melody from high
Listen, listen, songbirds cry
Beyond and all in Marys please
The curtains close, alas a bough
Of Willow sings in destiny
"I touch the spirit faraway still
I knew
Nights I sang with you
But to this room, unto the morrow
Sing I neither weep nor sorrow".

"How I wish
The peaceable concord, once-touch
To rule, to hope so much
For vanity all of kingdoms state
Of striving for kings, despair to a Queen
Or firstly woman so lastly hence
Here I
The black and temporal cloth shall fly"

"Then for I
Breathe scant more earthly reign
Let great and poor their mercy gain
From realms of men to heavens reply
So I reach to close my eyes with you
A lingered time in winters spread
Past leaded windows of this night
And why the tears, for my tomorrow?
Sing I, neither weep nor sorrow".

18 – Bharatavarsha

Cascades the snows and Himalayan kingship
A goddess Ganga Ma torrents to those
Whom vedic hymns have purified
Down mighty Siva, of ascetics hair
In greatest trickle, earth and plain
Release and cleanses, bathes and cures
All sins remove, devotees liberate
From evil multiplied three generations
The saints of sacred Ganges touch to find
Obtain desire, their last in waters of subcontinent.

Where glorious is the library of Purana
Celestial Song, supreme surrender
To Lord Krishna, last the Gita words
And Sanatana Dharmas flight
Samsaras journeying rebirth
Until their end of endless search
And Sikhs and beaten holy mystics teach
Disciples of those wise at temple gold.

The minarets of kingdom, founded, faded
That sing in swathe a furnace of the jewel
In grind of abject, streets of caste, bazaars
A Son of Brahma gorges down, North East
To crash in mighties reverent kiss
That reach and greet unto Assam.
To nimble Delta, fingers of a tide at Bay
A million gods and mantras, in old enchanters tale.

19 – Gypsy

Giants stand in guard of state
And yearning fall, sentries so well
So linger the daystar in beauty and blackness
November trees, the hand of Most High
When miles and miles were drift of perfume
The laziest column, nestling stead
Humming the Meadow grass, Speedwell and Pink
In flame to the fairy tale May once led.

The zest and pursuit, the webs spun of wonder
From home he came, light years and a day
Descent to a light shattered beck and all
New robes, new roof, new life for the green
When labour is passed and day afternoon
To make for the scatter, invasion of balm
And there beneath the dwellers so soon
Surrender to trespassers of wooded sleep.

Ephemeral they, of the ether – but stirred
Cloudlike a shadow, quiet a footstep
And sleep figures run for the real overheard
Dizzily seen, by an Acer he leapt
Let disbelief blink, let tresses discern
Less twenty yards there from Ash, untrue
In gypsy gold of a waking dream
Like figments that fled where another has led.

There, soulful aflood of sanguine form
Expressions to trickle, besotting in care
And to run bade coolness of the storm water surge
To verily follow through the Campion fair
Glimpse high to these, follow the track
Where shoes so fleet and small
Have pressed enriching turf fell back.
Gypsy gold, a monolith high.

20

The turmoil cry of youth evinced
In promised land, in heart of burst
A destiny stone, a telling soul
And temple hollow, call to the sky
Is ever there an Eden surpassing days of wine
Could sun recede, expressions leave this world
The cosmos ever treasure to relinquish this endearment kind
With hair of harvesttime, portent of the many still

This desirable pendant of halcyon seal
Fragrant the paths when elated time found.
In rye, in meander, immortals of time
In plane of all-forgotten and the aloe-oil sounds.
So lost is all speech for a rainbow prize
Would proffered be all wealth of the East
Unfailingly then could expressions despise
The breezed Summer copse, Wood Anemone of sighs.

Once there sat caravans of concert laughter hours
Travellers of no journey, asteroids course bereft
Under a final roof, their hundreds at the side
Move on without pain, leave the wistful haunt
Of a wind voice deep as the Prophets dirge
No substance, no harm, illusion remembered
As fruitage once withered, plucked dead – to the ground
And midwinters stretch where the gypsies have left.

21 – The Five

Ash that windward, leeward sights
His raiment keys to suspense light
Feathered dress, a gown depicts
The eloquent one without restrict.

Shrouded too the height of Elm
A mountains monolith, a realm
In happy canopy, the tall
And statures noble, arching fall.

Birch in fame ascends until
Wisps succumb to the earthly will
Skyline sketched and wistfully lingers
Above there white, fall ruby fingers.

Deserting once the new, the Plane
In population bears the stain
Of darkest breath, the city leaf
Where guarding girth by falling sheath.

And Whitebeam humble under the proud
Sits to the quickening call aloud
Upturned, grey, then end of May
The cream of majesties display.

22 – The Farewell

Goodbye could not for us wait, still
Hope springs always, hope we will;
So Lady span this surging crest
That signals closer, tears of test
Falling over the darkest edge
Of waters ever bear our pledge
To spur thee Lady on.

Rock thee gentle ship and arc
A cloud by painted topmast stark
Call, and sway, draw anchor away
So billow and plough tall ship this day
And leave in haunt the fairest face
Upon all oceans time or place
So constantly of thee.

Yet in long the now goodbye
White gulls a-rent their hollow cry
As we of echoed stains to shed
Were none such ever wrung, or said
More wouldst that in that New World say
For this, once our wedding day
Please Lord betide thee Lady.

Morning wreaks amongst the quay
And shadowed secrets cry to flee
In mornings blackest night of dearth
To westward, this poor side of earth
So are we bound, recall in leave?
How wealth and languor cross to grieve
As Lady thus do we.

So wealth that we within our souls
Pursue to the drummers beat and roll
And dismal, spectral silhouette
As phantom sails that scarcely let
Depart, but all thee left unwon will
Voyage hopes ascending sun, still
Then sail Lady on.

23 – Kanata

North Continental, quintessential
Sunrise to Emperor of seas
New found this land in giants sleep
Arose entrapment, tundra and trade
A hard born Old Worlds pioneer blood
New France from fire and beaver bought
Parlez Francais, and dear Quebecois
Where river narrows to the city of faith
Acadians of rugged Maritimes eked
And Recollet friars to a Royal Mount led
Baptised First Nations unto their fold
Algonquin spattered, by water crossed
Their saved to the true, to intrepid Champlain
Turned face to Iriquois's maple and mist
Fought the tough Mohawks upon lake shore
Cunning confederates painted, arraigned

When Abrahams Plains convulsed to change
The mad Wolfe scaled, De Montcalm fell
When Unities Act bound many as one
Races of shoulder to shoulder, The Higher,
The Lower, New French, Anglais
New religion and Old fought protagonists South
For a lasso of independents avert
Then in birch bark canoe, leather hide shoe
Trod dearly explorers trail to the prize
In claw and in rigour of Northwest's grip
Cold Nuvanuk to the Manitou Straits
Prairies of Princess Louise, way West
Assaulted the rich hills, Yukon snows
And Pathfinders meet at Columbia seas
Where the humble, peaceable and diverse stand
All lands within an equal land.

24 – Needless To Say

Needless to say, when everything
Said and done, tide has turned
But tide alone, who is sure to return
From mariners like us to sea
Like faith shipwrecked those cast adrift
When eloquence waters dash the edge
You were everything of Columbine
Revealed in supplicant rains of spring
After the January's snow-bound road
The clasp of make believe, therefrom
Out from theatre came reality
Many the daughters are fair, but you
Ascended higher than, so
Needless to say, besides you – none

25 – Writing On The Wall

Jayne, sad Jayne runs the January lane
Despairs road down the dirt pack snow
And after the sun of her winter feast, heard
That this must be, to us must be
And the writing was long before the wall
Belshazzers Feast, long end always next
Fleets to the path of her wedding day lost
And the long coated watcher stands without words.
Goodbye Jayne, know both we this song
Is sung in mists, we're here then gone
Casting adrift to a crushed walk home
And goodbye makes the finishing steps
So harder still for a story cursed
Deserted encounters were searching for trees
In desert, for whales in the forest.

Laughed at November rains to remember
That one way ride, the two player masks
Brought down at last in loves emptiest aisles
How badly was needed our secret ahead
Not there but where months were a lifetime – a day
Then smallest an image to the traffic unmoved
A load unassuaged, left back to the drifts
How streaked her eye shadow, how so not alone
How streaked is aback, see a figure, crushed reed
How windswept a burden, but so, how more so
To the one who has lowered the curtain, sad Jayne.

26 – Velvet

From deepest navy, arms adorn
In lace of ages, hands appear
To quill with tenderly new-born
Speed to the one 'though far but near.
With dance of eyes of faith that see
Unsparing quiver, light betrays
That one in the old room but she
Exist, for here one Queen in sway
Who reigns at state across beech wood
Alone, a ragged monarch rose
Taken, clasped, held to the flood
Breaks the quiet of a night
And to these oaken, panelled walls
That cannot hold, are the playful thrown
That rises Phoenix-like as future
Visions come, return her one – her own.

27 – All That Ventures

When spring of youth had fell, bewailed
That cry to the wild all flesh is grass
Long night had moaned, lake had froze
But over a canvas brush stroke blooms
There painted peace around her dew
There, the chosen always you.

Descried across the floor without face
We stepped to a crowd, eyes never down
We started a waltz in thunders applause
That never to end, the stars were our friends
A covenant under creation to all
And parted the night, we danced without pause.

All that ventures may never gain
But to us, to all in witness stand
In ripening sentient purpose make
A fledgling, our as one
When consummate discovery brings us
Here to you whom all spirit awakes.

A badge once of the White Rose spoke
That loyalty binds, this happy enslave
Of tyrants and heroes, the common
And glorious, pierces the more
Than fresh worlds conquered, for no land
Compares to the aura, this world now ours

28 – Quiet Eilidh

She leaves the long sash and waits amongst
Her expectancy blooms but so much
More a greater curtain falls, rendezvous
She knows not her age at this time of
The gathering and in a zenith star
Needs to be near, she carries not fear.
She would always be there as a new vow
Fulfilled in instance to crush many thorns
Far under and see no hard memory
No more those lonely refrains.

Quiet Eilidh was always long days again
That invited, called to her model hedge wall
In speech so tiny spoke in worlds
And came as colours of tribal days
To Indian skin house under the cosmos
To a blackest of nights November
Traffic and rains of lamplight without
Within, the place of a never to last
But always stranger, a soft brook below
Sad gravity ticks, last hours would flee.

Lost for once, was ever there found?
For her secret inner crystal tells
No turn, no judgement, no cloud but in share
Like Fall in a copper backwoods shade
Her wants to be wanted, arms realised
There in constancies warm winter room
Who could discern, who draws of this Well?
Of good hope in house and town garden hedge
Youths pensive hopes were wagons to our stars
And still now quiet Eilidh sings each, everyday.

29 – Scent of a Bottle

Past unconquered, hereto our perfume
Priceless of once where legends were born
The instant that from the opening, lent
The genies swirl and mirth, game afoot
To mirages of dearness, this smell of then, now
Artist strokes in nearness portraits
Scented canvasses faintly told
A piper's tune has played and rings to echo
Highland lochs so come, revisit
Our Indelibles, high of fairer isle
Come, that essence of the trade winds
Envelopes, heightens to the bottle fragrant
Sweet oracle of ambience tells all in his path
A finer tale, an always somethings
Richer palaces there bring down to knees
Somewhere in incarnations fingers
Caress of the eye or hand of time
Beckons in each turn, the never to pass
Are lights of a bay that flicker and stay.
From tiniest corners the message of glance
And she is there the invisible as
A spectre evinced in that look of faith
And squadrons arrayed or soldiers of jade
Then lift off the lid to a shimmering ago.

30 – To Find In The Ashes

That's found in the ashes we lost in the fire
Care Beneficent, the stay of all blows
And suffering, to quieten roaring of night
Of peace destitute in a vagabonds dream.
And loves avalanche moves all, everything
In highway there was right there was taught
Then you the becoming, the plentiful, and out
From night voice ruins on moorland tors
To spires, a beauteous city, steeped
Aloft our sanguine future lives.
A moribund grief, laid plainest to rest
In cinders disorder, our phoenix at last.

31 – Secret Heart

Not by food, by drink nor air
Is lonely purpose known, somewhere
The sometimes words inscribed are sown
A written fate of heart, a few
Or the many, of multitudinous know
That after the magic carpet ride
Would we be then who we've become
To know and to grasp beloved, without
A child eyes in a smallness time
Who lost is, the perennial fool.

To love, to grieve – in hurt to leave,
The one time they, of a travellers trade
To wonder what we might have known
To only have their wares – their being
With quiet haunches vanishing
Who'll always linger, last touched finger
As servants in a mansion lost
And who will endure the heartaches of fools.

32 – Wedding Day (The Crossing)

And so best wishes, this day of days
For the more, the untold numberless yet
Beyond, now our unwalked is crossed
To hope and new creation to
One flesh, one life, many miles the one step
Of our Great March celebrate
At last from that, the all we were
Now us, the all we'll be.
Though' said it changes always, yet
From desperate exiled ones ago
The savour of loving is found so
All more we are the same

When storms are mastering as one
There comes Pacific, Bay of Plenty.
And White Dress of the myriad
Woven, wedlocked, tiny, together.
Then Superlative one, our song
This which is Solomons
We live, we love, we suffer, become
Not us mere two, no, cord threefold.
This mansion build
Our hands unskilled
Then say, today – the best of all
Was this, our wedding day.

33 – Voyage (Who Will Mourn)

To go beyond, to stay the Way
In sight of an Almighties watch
Forgetful are we, no sad legacy
So part to each, one share, one being
One flesh, two bullets silver struck
A sun now warmer, as one reborn
Benevolence wed, of loyal love
Exalts in rhapsody, who will mourn?

So here are we to reside by promised
And armies of heavens that stoop to approve
Of passing, a little while order – who grieves?
Of the way we were, to this we'll be
Perennial our accomplished heart
The windsweep, the air of the voyage at dawn
Where great and our Lord of Faith can see
Our oceans whitecap – and who will mourn?

For exclusive discounts on Matador titles,
sign up to our occasional newsletter at
troubador.co.uk/bookshop